The Celebrity Cookbook

Introduction by Dinah Shore

Collected by Miss Shore
on behalf of
"Women For:"— a volunteer, non-partisan organization

PRICE STERN SLOAN publishers, INC.

LOS ANGELES

"How I brought all this to you without spilling a drop"

By Dinah Shore

Celebrities have a lesser known side to their lives, usually reserved for intimate friends and family. Sometimes it's revealed in what they like to cook. I really believe that many of them—in their private lives—see themselves as Walter Mittys in reverse...not as Sophia Lorens, or Jeanne d'Arcs or Ernest Hemingways, but as an ingenious domestic variety of Brillat Savarin in their own kitchens, able to concoct a superlative after-theater casserole or a spectacular soufflé on a moment's notice.

Many of my friends are well-known and unusually talented (in the kitchen, too) and I have thoroughly enjoyed eating the very special dishes they have cooked for me. In an effort to share my pride in my friends and their pleasure in cooking, I asked some of them to send me their favorite recipes. Gypsy Rose Lee parted with her superb formula for Portuguese Fish Chowder; Dean Martin revealed the secret ingredient in his noted Martinburger; Ralph Bunche forwarded his elegant Eggplant Provencal, Mrs. Lyndon Johnson, her famous Eggplant Creole. Three Beef Stroganoff experts—Natalie Wood, Gregor Piatigorsky and Mrs. Meredith Willson—sent their special methods of preparation. And there are others: some complicated, some as simple as Sandy Koufax's boiling water.

I am NOT a gourmet or a Cordon Bleu chef, but I do have a pretty fair knack in the kitchen with Paella Chilean, Beef Wellington or simply French Toast. I like my table to be attractive, my servings hearty and satisfying, a delight to the eye as well as knife and fork.

Just talking about food makes me long for my kitchen filled with ingredients, pots and pans, and platters. My predilection for gastronomy is justified by the very comforting words of George Bernard Shaw: "There is no love sincerer than the love of food." Fall in love yourself, as you join me in baking, boiling, roasting, stirring and eating these fabulous recipes from the MOST fabulous people.

contents

(Names listed alphabetically on page 12)

(Names listed alphabetically on page 12)

FIRST COURSES

ENTREES

DESSERTS

First Courses

dory langdon previn

CAVIAR IN ASPIC

4 to 6 ounces caviar
3 hard-boiled eggs
1 can mild chicken broth
2 envelopes unsweetened gelatin
bunch of watercress

dissolve gelatin in chicken broth for
a couple of minutes, then melt over heat.
scrape caviar into medium-sized ring mould.
spoon three or four tablespoons of broth over
caviar and shake mould until caviar is level
all around. place in icebox. separate hard-
boiled eggs, grate whites and yellows separately. when gelatin is set on the caviar,
take mould from icebox, sprinkle egg whites on
top of caviar, repeat the spooning and shak-
ing processes with more broth, again return
to icebox. when this layer has set, do the
same thing with the egg yolks. allow finally
to set firmly in icebox for an hour. now
unmould carefully onto a round or square
silver dish, decorate the center of ring
with just the tops of the watercress. serve
with hot toast, lemon, and small glasses of
vodka.

*the nice thing about this is that
you have caviar and its traditional accompaniments all in
one serving!*

Mrs. Andre' Previn

Phyllis Diller

RECIPE FOR GARBAGE SOUP

Back in the old days -- when cooking was done in the cave -- over a hot twig -- food was pure gold. The wheel was still "new" and I'll never forget one day when Aunt Hat looked at Uncle Ben during a rain storm --and at her stove under which only a few twigs were burning -- and she said: "You notice, the wet stuff puts out the hot stuff."

That brings us up to Garbage Soup. One of the rare delicacies of the civilized world, because it is an old French, Scandinavian, Yugoslavian, Icelandic, German, Dutch, Italian, Mohammedan, Irish, Jewish, Colored, custom... to have this big pot on the back of the stove, where you throw all the "usable" garbage.

Today, so many of the vitamins go down the drain. We in America, have the healthiest drains this side of the Mayo Clinic. Heavens! You throw the juice of cans -- the water you've cooked vegetables in, the meat in, etc.

Now, here's the way you make Garbage Soup:

You cozy up to your butcher (I hope he looks like Cary Grant, he probably doesn't) and ask him for a soup bone. This will thrill his body. Nobody asks for a soup bone. How many people own a Great Dane???

You take this home, and this is the beginning of Garbage Soup for the week, that is:

Fill a huge pot half full with water -- add salt, cracked pepper, salad lift, grated parmesan cheese, chili powder, a pinch of poultry seasoning (optional).
                                        Cont'd.

15

Garbage Soup cont.

Drop in the bone, forget the Great Dane, let him find
his own butcher, add:

<pre>
Fresh Chopped Onion
  "   "   Parsley
  "   "   Carrots
  "   "   Celery
  "   "   Potato
  "   "   Green Pepper
</pre>

" "
Simmer -- endlessly
" "
Then add - one large can of
tomatoes cut up
Two cans of kidney beans
" "

From then on -- all leftovers go into the soup --
with the exception of pickles and jello. Make sure
you chop leftovers fine and be sure to keep adding
juice from all cooking or cans opened...including
salad leftovers with dressing! Remember, when frying
any kind of meat, rinse skillet with water and throw
it in the Garbage Soup. Remember, anything boiled is
sterile, germless and the flavour is fantastic!

This is probably my biggest recipe! Love xxx phyllis

16

LORNE GREENE

Dear Dinah —

THIS IS ONE OF MY FAVORITE SALADS...........

One bunch of romaine
One bunch of watercress

The greens should be washed and well dried and torn
into bite size pieces.

Add two chopped hard cooked eggs
One cup of Julienne beets
One half cup of chopped green onions

Toss the above with plenty of olive oil and vinegar
dressing.

You may add a ripe avacado cut into bite size pieces,
but do not add until after the salad is pretty well
tossed so that the avacado does not get too broken up.

For french dressing we found that by using a mild white
vinegar, we can reduce the proportions of olive oil to vinegar
from the usual three to one to equal parts of each. This
turns out a fine dressing and cuts down on the calories.
We like olive oil, but you may substitute another salad oil
for part of it.

LORNE GREENE SALAD DRESSING...........

One half cup (scant) white vinegar
One half cup (generous) olive oil or part olive oil and part
                        other salad oil

contd.......

LORNE GREENE

One half teaspoon salt
One fourth teaspoon pepper
One half teaspoon dry mustard
One half teaspoon season salt
One half teaspoon monosodium glutamate

If you like garlic you may mash a clove into the dressing
or stab a small clove several times with a toothpick and
then spear the clove on the toothpick so you can remove it
easily from the dressing later.

I like to add about one half teaspoon of dry terragon———rubbing
this between the palms of your hands as you add it.

Shake well in a tightly capped jar. Remove the garlic and
taste the dressing for correct seasoning. Keep in the
refrigerator.

To this salad you may add a can of king crab or shrimp or other
seafood or bits of ham, cheese, tongue or any other variation
on a chef salad.

On a warm summer night this makes a just right meal with rolls
and fruit.

LORNE GREENE

18

MANDARIN ORANGE SALAD

1 pkg. of orange flavored gelatin

2 cups of apricot nectar

1 can of mandarin orange slices, drained

DRESSING

3 oz. pkg. of Philadelphia Cream Cheese

mayonnaise

celery chopped very fine

walnuts - chopped

Mildred M. Morse

(Mrs. Wayne Morse)
Oregon

MMM/sel

BOB CUMMINGS
1060 LAUREL WAY
BEVERLY HILLS, CALIFORNIA

BOB CUMMINGS FAVORITE

OYSTERS ROCKEFELLER:

24 Oysters on the half shell
1 cup butter
1/3 cup finely chopped parsley
1/4 cup finely chopped celery
1/4 cup finely chopped shallots
    or scallions
1/2 small clove of garlic, finely
    minced
2 cups chopped watercress
1/3 cup chopped fennel
1/3 cup fine soft breadcrumbs
1/4 cup - Pernod
Salt and freshly ground black
    pepper to taste

Preheat oven to hot(450)
Fill four tin pie plates with
rock salt and arrange six oysters on each. In a skillet heat
the butter, add parsley - celery -
shallots and garlic and cook about
3 minutes.
Pour this mixture into the container of an electric blender and
add the remaining ingredients.

Blend until sauce is thoroughly
pureed - about one minute.
Place one tablespoon of the sauce
on each oyster and spread to the
rim of the shell. Bake the Oysters
just until the sauce bubbles,
(about 4 minutes)...

Dear Dinah:

I rarely eat "rich" foods, but
psychologically, some times, its good
to remind your self that, "the
world is your oyster" so while you're
at it why not make it the richest
oyster.   Love Pat

PORTUGUESE FISH CHOWDER

Use equal amounts of potatoes, tomatoes and onions, all sliced very thin. Place in pressure cooker about ¼" olive oil, a layer of onions, a layer of tomatoes, a layer of potatoes. Sprinkle a tablespoon of parsley, a bit of salt, white pepper, about ¼ teaspoon very finely chopped garlic, a tablespoon of olive oil. Now repeat - one layer of onions, tomatoes, potatoes, parsley, etc., until pressure cooker is no more than 3/4 full. Cook at 15 pounds pressure for 3½ minutes. Reduce the pressure quickly by plunging pot in cold water. This may be served hot or chilled.

The Portuguese fishermen prepare this early in the morning aboard their fishing boats. It is placed over a small brazier, the lid weighted down with a sandbag. If the catch of the day includes delicacies that can be spared from the market, they are added to the vegetables. If not, the vege-tables are eaten without fish. It lends itself extremely well to any type of shellfish, snapper, or rolled up fish fillets secured with a toothpick.

Gypsy Rose Lee

Here is my recipe.

Potage Cressonière(Watercress Soup)
1 lb potatoes
1 teaspoon salt
1½ pints milk
one bunch of watercress
1 oz butter

                    Serves six to eight

Peel the potatoes, quarter them, and boil them in
salted water until tender. Drain, crush them with a
potato-masher, and when free from all lumps add the boiling
milk and salt. White the potatoes are cooking, wash and pick
the leaves off the watercress and chop roughly. Add to the
soup and cook for 5-6 minutes. Take off the fire and add the
butter. Pour into a hot tureen and serve.

This recipe has been chosen by me as a favorite recipe for
the simple, logical reason that I had it for the first time
on my first trip to the most beautiful city in the world,
Paris. It was a happy time, as it always is in Paris, so
I pass this on hoping that a flavor of the city of the
chestnut tress will be felt by all who have Potage
Cressonière.

                              Cordially,

                              Lauren Bacall

23

UMBRIAGO SALAD

For four salads:

Rub a large wooden sald bowl with
salt and one clove of garlic.
(Salt serves as an abrasive).

Mix Romaine (cold, dry and crisp)
with 1/4 teaspoon black pepper in
salad bowl. Then, form a bed with
1/4 cup croutons in center. Pour
over following dressing:

    1 tablespoon Worcestershire sauce
    1/4 Cup wine vinegar
    1/2 Tablespoon horseradish
    Juice of 1/2 lemon
    1/2 Tablespoon mustard
    1 dash tabasco

Toss lightly...then add a one-minute
egg and 1 Tablespoon chopped anchovies.
Toss salad again and sprinkle in two
Tablespoons parmesan cheese.

Jimmy Durante

Entrees

(A favorite recipe of the Secretary
of Agriculture, Orville L. Freeman)

Barbecued Beef Kabobs

1/2 cup olive oil or salad oil	1 pound tender lean beef cut in 1-1/2 inch cubes
1 teaspoon salt	2 large onions cut in wedges
1/2 teaspoon pepper	2 large tomatoes cut in wedges
1/2 teaspoon rosemary or oregano	8 ripe olives, pitted

Combine oil and seasonings. Add meat cubes and let stand
for several hours. Using four skewers, place 1/4 of meat
cubes, vegetables and olives in each skewer. Broil over
charcoal until brown or about 12 minutes, turning to brown
evenly. Four servings.

As most wives do, I prepare the pieces and do the marinating,
but the Secretary builds the fire and watches the cooking.

Jane C. Freeman

(Mrs.) Jane C. Freeman

Barbecuing is a way of life almost all year
round in California, and this Barbecued Lamb and
its accompanying herbed rice casserole, served
with a huge icy-cold Caesar salad and hot crispy
French bread, with fruit and cheese for dessert,
is one of my favorites for casual informal dining.

1. Have the butcher bone and butterfly a leg of
   lamb so that it will lie as flat as possible,
   reserving the bones for stock. (A seven-pound
   leg of lamb yields about five pounds of meat.)
   Make a marinade of 1 cup olive oil, 8 tbsps.
   wine vinegar, 2 crushed cloves of garlic, and
   1 tsp. salt. Place lamb in a shallow pan, skin
   side up, and pour over marinade, letting meat
   stand at least 4 hours and, preferably, over
   night, after slathering the skin side with
   plain prepared mustard.

2. Meanwhile, make a stock from the lamb bones,
   adding several cut stalks of celery with celery
   leaves, one whole onion, one green pepper cut
   in quarters, and salt and pepper to taste,
   simmering slowly for several hours. When done,
   remove bones and strain, putting aside for later.

cont.

3. Build a very hot bed of coals and, when ready to barbecue, place lamb on grill, mustard side down, about five inches from the coals. This sears the meat and seals in the juices. When brown on one side, turn. I find a five-pound piece of meat takes approximately one hour, but I test for doneness after about forty-five minutes by slicing through the thickest part of the meat. The lamb should not be well done, but still faintly pink in the center, and very juicy. When done, slice thinly a la Chateaubriand, and serve on a heated platter.

4. Just prior (or earlier in the day, if you like) to putting the meat on the barbecue, soften one cup chopped onion in $\frac{1}{4}$ cube of butter in a heavy skillet (about 5 minutes). Add 1 cup uncooked white rice and brown slightly, stirring occasionally. Add two tbsps. parsley and two tbsps. each thyme, oregano and rosemary, and 1 tsp. salt, stirring to meld flavors. When ready to cook the meat, transfer rice mixture to a covered casserole and add three cups boiling stock. Cover and place in 300° to 325° oven at the same time you begin to barbecue lamb. All liquid should be absorbed by the rice, and both the rice and lamb will be ready for serving at the same time.

Happy Barbecuing,

Frank Sinatra

BEEF STROGANOFF

$1\frac{1}{2}$ pounds sirloin steak, cut in $\frac{1}{2}$ inch strips
$\frac{1}{4}$ cup flour
1 teaspoon salt
2 small onions, chopped fine
$\frac{1}{2}$ pound mushrooms, cut in pieces
1 clove garlic, chopped fine
3 tablespoons butter
2 tablespoons flour
1 cup beef bouillon (canned)
1 tablespoon Worcestershire sauce
1 cup sour cream

Rice or noodles

Roll steak in $\frac{1}{4}$ cup flour and salt. Pan fry onions,
mushrooms and garlic in fat for 5 minutes. Add steak
and brown evenly, then remove meat, onions and mushrooms from pan. Combine 2 tablespoons flour with
drippings, in the pan. Add bouillon and Worcestershire
sauce. Cook until thickened. Add sour cream and heat
slowly until gravy simmers, (do not boil!). Add beef
and vegetables and heat for a few minutes.

Serve on hot cooked rice or noodles. Makes 4 to 5
servings.

Gregor Piatigorsky

29

Rini Willson

BEEF STROGANOFF (4 Servings)

2 lbs. round steak cut in small narrow strips about
   1-1/2 inches
1 medium sized Onion
Seasoning to taste - include pepper, onion salt,
   garlic salt
1 can of Tomato Sauce (smallest can)
1/4 to 1/2 lb. Mushrooms (fresh or canned)
2 tsps. Worcestershire Sauce
1 pint Sour Cream
Sprinkle of Paprika

Method: Chop onions and brown in butter or oil (as
much butter or oil as desired) in deep skillet.
Put meat on top of onions and mix
Cover skillet and simmer for about 1 hr. 15 mins.
Put in mushrooms (cut in quarters if large)
Mix in seasonings, Worcestershire Sauce, Paprika and
   Tomato Sauce
Simmer again until meat is tender
About 15 mins. before serving fold in sour cream
Serve on bed of Pilaff

* * *

Mrs. Meredith Willson

Beef Stroganoff

2 lbs. sirloin beef cut in thin strips
3/4 cup butter
3 medium chopped onions
1/2 lb. can button mushrooms
1 cup tomato juice
1/2 cup water
3/4 cup sherry
1 cup of sour cream
Salt
Pepper
Flour

Dredge meat in flour. Brown quickly in half
of the butter. Remove meat from skillet and
add remaining butter. Add onions and mushrooms.
Cook 5 minutes. Add meat, sprinkle salt and
pepper. Add tomato juice, sherry, and water.
Bring slowly to boil. Cover and simmer until
tender - about 1½ hours. Just before ready
to serve, stir in sour cream. Serve on boiled
rice.

Natalie Wood

Every time I think of this recipe, I get homesick
for our other home in Mexico, but in the meantime I eat
and enjoy........

FRIJOLES NEGROS ESTILO RANCHERO DE MORELOS or

RANCH STYLE BLACK BEANS

2 lbs. black beans

2 lbs. Pork Loin, cut up as for stew

1 Medium Onion, diced

1 Chile (or any variety small red or green hot pepper)

Salt

Diced Radishes

Corriandor

Lemon Juice

Soak beans in cool water overnight (at least 8 hours).
Drain, and cover again with cool water. Boil and
simmer until the skins wrinkle. Add chopped onion,
cut up meat, chopped chile and a touch of salt.
When meat is well cooked, serve in soup plate, top
each plate with chopped radish and corriandor and
a squeeze of lemon over all. Recommended with a side
order of Tequila Añejo.

Budd Schulberg.

CARL REINER

BOEUF EN DAUBE MRS. REINER

Found this recipe sometime ago in the New York Times and
have eaten it twenty-seven times since then. I recommend
it only for those people who love delicious things. I
call it "Boeuf En Daube Mrs. Reiner" because she's the
one who stole the recipe.

3 pounds chuck or stewing beef cut into two-inch cubes
1 ½ cups red wine
¼ cup cognac
2 tablespoons peanut oil
Salt and freshly ground black pepper to taste
½ teaspoon thyme
1 bay leaf
1 large onion, coarsely chopped
2 cloves garlic, crushed
2 cups scraped, thinly sliced carrots
½ cup coarsely chopped celery
½ pound sliced lean bacon, each slice cut in half
Water
Flour for dredging
2 ½ cups Italian plum tomatoes or fresh, ripe tomatoes
cored, peeled and chopped
2 cups thinly sliced mushrooms
2 cups beef stock, fresh or canned.

1. Place the beef in a large mixing bowl and add the
wine, cognac, oil, salt, pepper, thyme, bay leaf, onion,
garlic, carrots and celery. Cover and refrigerate three
hours or longer.
2. Preheat the oven to 350 degrees.
3. Place the bacon in a saucepan and add water barely
to cover. Simmer five minutes and drain.
4. Line a heatproof casserole with three or four pieces
of bacon. Drain the beef and reserve the marinade.
5. Dredge each cube of beef in flour and shake to
remove excess. Arrange a layer of beef in the casserole,
add a layer of the marinated vegetables, a third of the
tomatoes and a third of the mushrooms. Continue making
layers until the ingredients are used, ending with
vegetables and bacon. Sprinkle all with salt and pepper.
Add beef broth and enough of the marinade to cover. Cover
and bring to a boil on top of the stove. Place in oven
and bake 15 minutes. Reduce heat so that casserole barely
simmers and cook til meat is fork tender. Yield: Six
servings.

Carl Reiner

33

ARLENE FRANCIS

Brookforest Eggs

2 Dozen eggs
1 Med green pepper, diced
½lb. fresh mushrooms, sliced and sauteed,
or 1 small can sliced mushrooms
3 cups leftover baked ham, or canned pressed
ham, diced
1lb. Cheddar cheese, sliced
salt and pepper

Break six eggs into a mixing bowl and
beat lightly with a fork. Spill a little of
the beaten eggs into a large, lightly buttered casserole. Sprinkle the bottom of the
casserole with ¼ of the ham, green pepper
and mushrooms. Break three or four of the
unbroken eggs into the casserole, being careful to keep them whole with the yolks unbroken. Space them as far apart as possible.
Salt and pepper to taste. Completely cover with
slices of cheese, and pepeat the process,
layer on layer. Finish with a top layer of
cheese, and sprinkle with paprika. Bake at
least 1½ hrs in 350 oven. A serving spoon
stuck into the casserole will stand upright
when the dish is cooked. Let stand for five
minutes and serve.
Serves 12

34

ZERO MOSTEL

Calf's-Foot Jelly

I am mad about jelly cooking, so here's a
great English dish that's good when you're
sick and better when you're healthy. Other
names for Calf's-foot Jelly are Pitcha,
Drelle, Studen, Cholodetz. No matter what
you call it, a pleasant gas stays with you
all day.

The ingredients:
  1 calf's foot
  4 pints water
  1 bay leaf
  3 cloves garlic,
    chopped up well

  2 teaspoons salt
  Pepper to taste
  1/4 teaspoon all-
    spice
  1/4 pint white wine
  3 hardboiled eggs

You bring the calf's foot to a boil and
skim it. Put in the bay leaf and simmer it
a good three hours. Then remove all the
meat and gristle from the bone. Chop it up
and add to the strained liquid. Add the
other ingredients and boil for a further
15 minutes. Slice the eggs and put them
in the bottom of a very decorative dish.
Put in the gristle and pour the liquid
slowly over it. Then chill it and enjoy!

Zero Mostel

CASA LADERA
1700 COLDWATER CANYON DRIVE
BEVERLY HILLS, CALIFORNIA

CHICKEN "CASA LADERA"

2 Fryers, cut up and dusted with salt, paprika. Saute and brown in 1/4 lb. butter. Place in casserole with 1 cup chicken broth and 1 cup white wine.

Cook in 300 degrees oven until tender (about 40 min.
                                              covered)

Saute in butter 1 lb. fresh mushrooms

Saute in another pan 1 lb. chicken livers

Combine liquid from 2 pans, add 2 tbsp. flour

Arrange mushrooms and chicken livers on top of chicken in casserole, pour over liquid, sprinkle with chives.

Serve with rice and French bread.

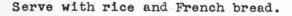

36

Chicken Ala Doroté

(Chicken Breasts with Sour Cream and Capers)

3 breasts of chicken, boned	salt and pepper to taste
¼ pound butter	paprika
2 large onions	1 pint sour cream
1 bunch celery	1 bottle of capers

(Makes Six Servings)

Heat oven to 350°F. Cover bottom of baking pan with sliced celery and onions. Sprinkle salt and pepper over ingredients. Then salt and pepper breasts of chicken that have been cut in half. Place chicken on top of celery and onions and pour melted butter over all. Sprinkle lightly with paprika and cover with foil. Bake for 45 minutes. Remove foil and brown.

Remove chicken and strain gravy, putting it aside. (Gravy will be of thin consistency.) Discard celery and onions and return chicken to pan.

Mix gravy with sour cream until it reaches the consistency of white sauce. Add capers and pour over chicken. Bake in slow oven until chicken is tender.

* * *

Acknowledgement due
our cook, Mrs. Dorothy Davis

Miriam Schary

(Mrs. Dore Schary)

Havoc Hurry Chicken

1 nice frying chicken or as many breasts
   as needed.
1 Med. bottle stuffed olives.. drained.
Quarter lb. butter
1 Pint sour cream
Onions as desired

Melt butter...golden the onions..add olives.
Remove and keep warm while frying chicken.
Remove chicken when golden..
Add sour cream to butter ..blend well.
Add olives and onions...blend well..pour
over chicken....Wowsie...Dowsie!

Shouldnt take over half and hour.
Should put ten pounds on you.

Best !

June Havoc

JIMMY'S CHILE

My husband, Jimmy, tried cooking exactly once...when we were first married, I became ill with the flu and the doctor suggested that he boil me an egg...which he did... with no water in the pot! Just an egg, a pot and a flame! The explosion was violent...the aroma no aid to my condition...and the expense of scraping, scrubbing and painting the kitchen was so great that he has been barred from that part of the house ever since...a penalty that does not upset him.

Anyway, this is his favorite dish. It bears no resemblance to Mexican or Texas Chili. It's fast, easy and a great solution to the false hunger the morning after.

    1 Lb. Ground Round
    1 Medium Onion - Chopped
    1 Large Green Pepper - Chopped
    2 Cloves Garlic (run through press)
    1½ Cans No. 2 Can Kidney Beans (drained)
                (Save juice for soup)
    1½ Cans No. 2 Can Whole Tomatoes
    1½ tsp. Salt
    3 Whole Cloves
    1 Bay Leaf
    3 tbsp. Bacon Fat
    3 tbsp. Good, Strong, Fresh Chili Powder

Brown onion, chopped peppers, garlic and meat in bacon fat till brown and crumbly. Add tomatoes, beans, salt, cloves bay leaf and chili powder. Bring to boil...then cook over a very low flame for about 2½ hours, stirring occasionally. To thicken (we like it soupy so we can dunk), leave lid off till it reaches thickness you desire. We have added one or all of these at one time or another.

    Leftover Stew Meat (or cook some especially for this
                                            dish)

    Toasted Saltines
    Sour Cream (Lots of it mixed in and heated to boiling)

If you use all of these, it is a marvelous party dish, which we then serve over rice. If you don't think it tastes like chili, you're probably right. But I've never been able to come up with a better name for it. Whatever you care to call it...we wish we had some right now!!!

Henny Backus -

COQ AU VIN

The extra steps that make this version so good include
browning the chicken and vegetables, adding brandy
(flamed as it is put into the stew) and, most crucial
of all, removing the finished chicken and vegetables
from the sauce to about half its former quantity by a
quick boil.

This last intensifies the flavor of the sauce
immeasurably. "Beurre manié" is added to make the
sauce a little richer still – and thicken it slightly.

3 chicken breasts, halved

6 chicken legs

24 medium mushrooms

24 tiny white onions

1/4 cup butter

1/4 lb. thick sliced bacon

1 teaspoon sugar

1 clove garlic, minced

1/4 cup brandy

2 cups dry red wine

1 can chicken broth

1/2 teaspoon thyme leaves

1 bay leaf

1 tablespoon dry parsley

1 tablespoon butter

1 tablespoon flour

1/4 cup water

Dry the chicken pieces thoroughly and sprinkle them with
salt and pepper. Wash the mushrooms and remove the stems.

Peel the onions. To do this effortlessly, drop them
into a pot of boiling water. Count to 10 slowly, then
drain the onions and run under cold water. The skin
will slip off between your fingers. Cut bacon into
half-inch pieces and cook in butter in a large Dutch
oven or casserole until lightly browned. Remove bacon
and drain. Pour half of the accumulated fat into a
second large pan or skillet so you can use two pans
for browning the chicken.

Add the chicken to fat, skin side down, without
crowding. Cook it over medium heat until lightly
browned on both sides. As pieces brown, remove them
and add more. When all are browned, set aside.

From now on you will work only with the heavy casserole
dish. Put the onions into it, add sugar and cook,
stirring until onions are lightly browned. Then brown
mushrooms and garlic. Put the chicken back in the pot
and pour most of the brandy in over it. Retain about
one tablespoonful and put it into a ladle. Light the
brandy in the ladle and pour it, flaming, into the
casserole to ignite the rest of the brandy. When you
do this, stand back, as the whole casserole will flame
up instantly. When the flame dies, add the wine, broth,
water and herbs. Cover pan and simmer for 30 minutes,
or until the chicken is tender. Remove chicken, bacon,
mushrooms and onions.

Bring stock left in pan to a broil, skimming off fat
as it rises. Boil stock rapidly for about five minutes
or until liquid is reduced to about two cups. Mix one
tablespoon butter and flour together thoroughly with
a fork and stir this beurre manié into the sauce. Cook
until the sauce thickens. Strain and pour over chicken.

If you are making the Coq Au Vin ahead, strain the sauce
into a separate container and store it in the refrigerator.

To reheat, place covered chicken in 325 degree oven
for about 30 minutes. Arrange on platter. Meanwhile,
reheat sauce separately and pour over chicken. Serve
with rice that has been fluffed up with butter and
parsley.

CORN BEEF A LA SOPHIE

In the morning, take a large piece of corn
beef that has not been too pickled. Cook in
boiling water with celery, onions and carrots
for 5 to 6 hours until it is tender.

Remove from stock and let cool. Remove as
much fat as possible. 50 minutes before
you plan to serve dinner, make a glaze:
take one jar of Gulden's mustard and coat
the corn beef, then cover this with 1 lb.
box of brown sugar. Put in oven for 45 minutes
until corn beef is completely glazed.

Sophie Gimbel

CREPES MAISON

(Pancakes filled with curried
chicken and lobster)

Serves 8

1 jar chutney
1 five-pound chicken, roasted (remove skin and cut
     chicken into bite-sized pieces.)

2 one and one-half pound lobsters, boiled (cut
     meat into bite-sized pieces.)

Mix chicken and lobster meat together

Batter

4 large eggs
1/4 teaspoon salt
1 1/2 cups club soda
1 1/2 cups flour
1 bar and 1 tablespoon butter, clarified

Clarify 1 bar and 1 tablespoon butter. Keep warm
over hot water. Break 4 large eggs into an electric
blender, add 1/4 teaspoon salt, 1 1/2 cups club
soda, 1 1/2 cups flour and 3 tablespoons clarified
butter. Blend for a second or two, or until smooth
and free from lumps. Heat a small frying pan and
when it is hot, brush it lightly with clarified
butter. Pour 2 tablespoons batter onto center of
pan and cook crepes on both sides very quickly.
Repeat until all batter is used, brushing pan with
clarified butter between times.

Keep finished crepes warm.   **cont.**

Curried Sauce

4 medium-sized apples
2 large onions
6 stalks celery
1/4 lb. butter
4 tablespoons flour
4 tablespoons curry powder
4 cups chicken broth, heated
1/2 cup light cream

Peel, core and cut up 4 medium-sized apples.
Peel and chop 2 large onions. String, wash and
chop 6 stalks of celery. Cook apples, onions
and celery together in 6 tablespoons butter
until they are soft and lightly brown (10 to 15
minutes).

Add 2 additional tablespoons butter and 4 tablespoons flour mixed with 4 tablespoons curry powder.
Stir and add 4 cups of clear, hot chicken broth
and simmer for another 30 minutes, stirring
occasionally.

Cool slightly and run through blender. Add 1/2
cup light cream and stir well.

Put chicken and lobster pieces into curried sauce
and reheat. Fill crepes with chicken and lobster
mixture, roll up and arrange on warm serving
dish. Pour curried sauce over all. Serve with
chutney passed separately.

Dorothy Rodgers

Mrs. Richard Rodgers

Mrs. Hubert H. Humphrey

3216 Coquelin Terrace, Chevy Chase, Maryland 20015

DINNER-IN-A-DISH

4 Tbsp. shortening

1 med. onion, chopped

2 green peppers, diced

1½ lb. hamburger

1½ tsp. salt

¼ tsp. pepper

2 eggs

2 c. whole kernel corn (or 1 #2 can)

4 med. tomatoes (or 1 #2 can)

½ c. cracker crumbs

Put shortening in heavy skillet and lightly fry pepper and onion for three minutes. Add seasonings. Remove from fire, stir in eggs and mix well. Put one cup of corn in casserole, then half of meat mixture, a layer of sliced tomatoes. (If using canned vegetables — drain off juice). Repeat layers and cover with crumbs. Dot with bits of butter. Bake in moderate oven (375°) 1 hour.

Muriel Humphrey

45

MRS. LYNDON B. JOHNSON'S RECIPE FOR:

EGGPLANT CREOLE

2 small eggplant	1 1/2 cups fresh
4 strips bacon	bread crumbs
1/2 cup minced onion	1 cup sauteed mushrooms
1/2 cup minced green pepper	1 tablespoon Dry mustard
4 cups drained canned tomatoes	Salt and pepper
1/2 cup diced celery	Grated Parmesan cheese

Wash and dry eggplant. Cut in half lengthwise. Scoop
out pulp and chop (leave shell about 1/4 in. thick). Mince
bacon and heat in a skillet. Add onion and green pepper
and saute until bacon is done. Add chopped eggplant,
tomatoes and celery.

Simmer until eggplant is tender.

Beat with a whip or fork until all ingredients are well
blended. Add half the bread crumbs and dry mustard
and beat until well blended.

Season with salt and pepper.

Fold in the mushrooms. Fill eggplant shells, dust generously
with cheese and top with remainder of bread crumbs. Dribble
a little melted butter over the crumbs and put eggplants in
a pan with a little water in the bottom and bake in 350 oven,
15 to 20 minutes or until eggplant is heated through and the
crumbs lightly browned.

Egg Plant Provencale

Step 1

Choose firm Egg Plants, wash and peel, cut into 1/2 inch thick slices, season with salt, pepper and paprika. Sprinkle over them a mixture of fine chopped parsley, garlic and bread crumbs, then shake a few drops of oil over slices, place on a lightly greased pie plate or baking pan and grill in oven until lightly browned and tender.

Step 2

Cut medium size Tomato in half, season with salt and pepper, sprinkle with a mixture of fine chopped parsley, garlic and bread crumbs, then shake a few drops of oil over halves, place on a lightly greased pie plate or baking pan and grill in oven until lightly browned and tender.

Step 3

When serving, place grilled Tomato on top of Egg Plant.

Ralph J. Bunche

Ralph J. Bunche

Nanette Fabray Mac Dougall

When a woman loves to cook, but works outside
the home, there comes that desperate day when
she runs out of frozen casseroles, and can't
bear the thought of another steak or chop, but
needs a quick dinner. This one is marvelous
and practically fool proof, and takes twenty
minutes from start to finish.

FILLET OF FISH AND CHEESE
(serves 4)
4 Fillets of sole (or any sweet fish)
Salt and freshly ground pepper to taste
4 tablespoons butter
½ cup grated Parmesan cheese (about)
½ cup bottled clam juice (about)

Wash the fillets in lemon water and dry. Season
with salt and pepper. Melt butter in a skillet
and saute the fish on both sides. Sprinkle with
the cheese and add enough clam juice to come to
the edge of the cheese on the fish without cover-
ing the fish. Cover pan and cook over low heat
5 minutes. The fish can be served like this.
* * * * * * * * * * * * * * * *

However I like to remove the fish to a warm
platter or the dinner plates. Then scrape the
sides and bottom of the skillet to loosen the
'goodies' stuck there, add ½ teaspoon of flour
and a tablespoon of cream, and cook the gravy
until it thickens slightly, pour over the fish
and serve. MMMMMMMMMM!

Nanette F. MacDougall

48

THE CAROLINA ISRAELITE

THE MOST WIDELY QUOTED PERSONAL JOURNAL IN THE WORLD
HARRY GOLDEN, EDITOR

HOLISHKAS
(STUFFED CABBAGE)

2 pounds lean, raw beef, chopped
Salt and pepper to taste
1 cup cooked rice
2 cans tomato sauce
2 cans tomato paste
1 onion, chopped
1/2 cup vinegar
2 cups water
1/3 cup sugar
1 cup raisins
16-18 ginger snaps
Large cabbage leaves

Soak the cabbage leaves in hot water a few minutes to make them less brittle. Season the meat lightly with salt and pepper. Add rice. Roll a portion of the meat mixture in each leaf. Place them in a large low pan with the rest of the ingredients and let them simmer until the cabbage is tender and well browned. Serves 6 to 8.

Harry Golden

PLEASE REPLY TO BOX 2505, CHARLOTTE NORTH CAROLINA 28201 / TELEPHONE 375-6624

IRVING WALLACE
308 SOUTH BRISTOL AVENUE
LOS ANGELES, CALIFORNIA 90049

HAMBURGER PUDDING A LA I.W.

I would love to say that I have a secret recipe for preparing Chateaubriand sauce Bearnaise to be enjoyed with a glass of Gevrey-Chambertin '59. But in truth, when it comes to food, I am a person with a Rolls-Royce appetite and a Chevrolet taste. My favorite entree is a succulent Hamburger taken with a chilled and vintage year Coca Cola.

1   But do not be deceived by the simplicity of the Hamburger. The preparation of this traditional serving of chopped beef can be as varied as Man himself. I have enjoyed favorite Hamburgers of every nationality - from the incredibly delicious Hamburger-Steaks of the Royal Danieli Roof Terrace and of Harry's Bar in Venice to those of La Tour D'Argent and the Champs Elysees Pam-Pam Restaurant in Paris. While these are deserving of a gourmet's palate, the very best version of Hamburger I have enjoyed has been one served at our own dinner table in West Los Angeles. For a decade and a half, this special Hamburger dish has been a cherished family secret. But now, out of charity for those famished ones of simple taste like myself, the secret stands revealed:

The Origins of Hamburger Pudding a la I.W., as I like to call it, are lost in French history. The basic recipe, since refined, was brought to us

50

Hamburger Pudding cont.

by a clever and inventive French housekeeper-cook
who came to our employ from a suburb of Paris. The
secret recipe is as follows:

    The basic ingredients: 1 small onion,
                             4 large potatoes,
                             3/4 lb. ground meat.

    The preparation: Chop the onion, but not too
finely. Brown the shreds in butter. Add all of the
ground beef. Into the mixture, a dash of salt, a
dash of pepper, a dash of All-Seasoning. Leave
uncovered, and cook slowly for 20 minutes. As
you cook, continue to break up the ground meat.
Now, having cooked the potatoes, mash them
tenderly, evenly, adding a modest portion of
milk. Take out a glass casserole. Fill the
bottom with a thin layer of mashed potatoes. On
top of this, spread the meat mixture. Then, atop
this, spread another layer of the mashed potatoes.
Place the casserole in a broiler and brown the
pudding slowly. About 40 minutes, low flame, will
produce a deep crust. Present the dish steaming
hot, serving the pudding in slices or scoops.

    Voila! From family, from dinner guests,
I promise you ecstatic cluckings and love.

                    A votre sante!
                    Irving Wallace

LAMB STEW RUMANIA

3 Lbs. Shoulder Lamb (cut to stew size)
2 Lbs. Breast Lamb   "   "   "   "
3 Cloves Garlic
10 Yellow Onions
2 Lbs. Potatos
Fresh Dill
Paprika

Cover the bottom of a stew pot with 5 quartered
onions. Next place half of mixed lamb over
onions. Press in one clove of garlic, add sprig
of dill, sprinkle with paprika.

With remainder of ingredients repeat process -
a layer of onions, a layer of lamb, a clove of
garlic, sprig of dill and sprinkle with paprika.

Cover pot and place over a slow flame. After
fifteen minutes, begin periodic stirring. After
one hour, press in last clove of garlic and add
quartered potatos. When potatos are cooked,
remove from fire and serve. Will serve six.

Hal March

Dear Dinah Shore

I am usually asked for Recipes
for living and loving rather Than
for Recipes for Cooking.
IT is Therefore unusually pleasing
To be invited To This culinary
symposium _
Here is my simple contribuiTion:
1) Mushrooms
2) Olive oil flavored with garlic
3) Parsley
    clean mushrooms — chop mushrooms
and parsley very small and mix with
oil; or, even quicker, put ingredients in
                    cont.

Oesterizer - however, if you do so, dont liquefy, only chop. And that is all there is to it. The rawness of the mushrooms gives this mixture a very earthy, yet refined, flavor. Be very discreet with the garlic - it is a powerfull elixir!

You can use this mixture in a variety of ways: with steamed rice or spaghetti - spread on veal scaloppine, or, if you put it in a strainer for a few minutes and let the oil strain out, it is delicious on toast for a light lunch or hors-d'oeuvre.

With this raw mushrooms Recipe you can nonchalantly mix, in your conversation, The Magic Mushroom. The more imaginative of your guests will soon begin to feel that you have indeed mixed a bit of magic in your earthy food ... and maybe you have!

Cordially (anna Archera Huxley

Dean Martin

MARTIN BURGERS

1 lb. ground beef
2 oz. bourbon---chilled

Preheat a heavy frying pan and sprinkle
bottom lightly with table salt. Mix meat,
handling lightly, just enough to form into
four patties. Grill over medium-high
heat about 4 minutes on each side.

Pour chilled bourbon in chilled shot glass
and serve meat and bourbon on a TV tray.

SWEDISH MEAT BALLS à la ALMA
(for 12)

1-1/2 pounds ground beef (chuck or round steak)
1 pound lean pork
1 pound lean veal

Have butcher put meat through grinder twice. Mix together well in a large bowl.

Grate into bowl: 1 small onion
                     1 piece nutmeg (or 1 tsp. powdered
                       nutmeg)
                     1 whole allspice (about 1/2 tsp.)
Add: salt and pepper to taste
                     1 dash Tabasco
                     3 egg yolks
                     1/2 cup very rich bouillon
                     about 1/2 cup cream

Knead thoroughly until very light and fluffy, then roll into small balls.

Brown in butter until golden and place balls in a large pot. Make gravy of the drippings by adding 1 or 1-1/2 tbsp. flour, and about 2 cups of bouillon (or bouillon mixed with vegetable stock) and a little cream. Pour over balls in the pot, cover, and simmer very slowly 15 or 20 minutes.

Serve with rice or buttered noodles.

> My Finnish cook, Alma says that the secret
> of this recipe is to use very rich bouillon
> stock and vegetable stock brewed in your
> own kitchen.

Kitty Carlisle Hart

Edgar Bergen

SWEDISH MEAT BALLS

1 lb. ground round steak

2 Tablespoons minced onion

1/3 cup bread crumbs

1/2 cup milk (or half and half)

1 egg

Salt and pepper to taste.

Edgar Bergen

ONE WEST SIXTY SEVENTH STREET
NEW YORK

Recipe by Fannie Hurst

MEAT BALLS IN WINE SAUCE

1 lb. ground chuck or round
1 large apple, peeled and shredded
1 egg slightly beaten
1¼ teaspoon salt
1/8 teaspoon pepper

Combine and shape into balls about an inch in diameter.

Heat 4 tablespoons salad oil in skillet. Add meat balls and
¼ cup chopped onions. Cook over medium heat about 10 minutes,
until the meat is lightly browned on all sides.

WINE SAUCE

Combine: ¾ cup Burgundy wine
          ¼ "   water
          2 8 ounce cans tomato sauce
          ⅛ teaspoon basil
          ¼ "   rosemary
          ¼ "   sugar

Pour over meat balls. Cover and simmer 15 minutes.

* * * * * * * * *

Serve over spaghetti. May be prepared in advance. Serves 4.

Fannie Hurst

58

MEAT LOAF

2# chopped chuck
½# each, pork and veal (lean)
2 eggs, beaten lightly
1½ cup Pepperidge Farm stuffing
½ cup catsup and fill rest of cup to brim
   with warm water
1 pkge.Lipton Onion Soup mix
Salt & pepper to taste
Mold into loaf
½ cup red wine poured over loaf and let soak
Mushroom caps & olives on top

Bake in 350° oven until brown, approximately
45 minutes.
1 small can tomato sauce with a little water
added. Pour over loaf after baking, then put
back in oven (turned off) for about 15 minutes,
or until it bubbles.

Shirley Booth

GERTRUDE BERG
829 PARK AVENUE
NEW YORK 21, N.Y.

Meat Stuffed Prunes

24 large unsweetened prunes

6 tablespoons shortening

1 onion, chopped

1/2 lb. ground beef

1/2 cup crushed, canned pineapple drained

4 tablespoons lemon juice

3 tablespoons brown sugar

3 onions, sliced thin

1 cup canned tomato sauce

4 gingersnaps crushed

1 1/2 spoons salt

1/4 teaspoon freshly ground black pepper

Soak the prunes overnight in water to cover. (This step may be omitted if
the pre-soaked variety is used.) Pit very carefully. Melt 2 tablespoons of
shortening in a skillet. Add chopped onion and saute for 5 minutes stirring
frequently. Add the beef, pineapple, 1 tablespoon of lemon juice, and one
tablespoon of brown sugar. Cook over slow heat for 10 minutes stirring
frequently. Stuff the prunes with the mixture. Melt the remaining shortening in a saucepan, saute the sliced onions in it for 10 minutes stirring
frequently. Add the tomato sauce, gingersnaps, salt, pepper, and remaining
lemon juice and sugar. Add the prunes carefully, open side up. Cover and
cook over low heat for 25 minutes. Correct seasoning. The sauce should be
both sweet and sour.

Serve as an accompaniment to meat or poultry dishes or as a main course
with potatoes.

Meat Stuffing for
Fowl and Pies

1-1/2 pounds veal ground together with
1-1/2 pounds pork
  1/2 cup celery chopped fine
2   medium onions chopped fine

Cook over medium heat until pork is well done. Drain fat before adding 2 cups mashed potato--a little at a time in order not to have dressing runny. Season with 1 table-spoon salt, 1/4 teaspoon pepper, 1 teaspoon cinnamon and 1/4 teaspoon cloves. (No additional fat other than from pork is needed.) Taste and adjust seasoning (this is the tricky part). Cool and stuff fowl or make meat pie. Pie is delicious served with giblet gravy.

Lawrence F. O'Brien

61

From the kitchen of Edward G. Robinson

BAKED NOODLES

LARGE PKG. WIDE NOODLES
1 GREENPEPPER
2 LG. ONIONS (CHOPPED FINE)

BROWN PEPPER AND ONION IN BUTTER, SALT AND
PEPPER.

COOK 3 LBS. GROUND ROUND WITH ABOVE FOR
20 MINS.

CUT FINELY 1 LB. CHEDDAR CHEESE, PUT IN WITH
MEAT.

WHEN FAIRLY MELTED, MIX IN 2 CANS TOMATO SOUP
2 CANS TOMATO SAUCE

MIX ALL ABOVE WITH *cooked* NOODLES.

PUT IN COVERED PYREX IN HOT OVEN 30 MINS.(400)

TURN OVEN DOWN TO 325, COOK AS LONG AS YOU
WANT...30 MINS.

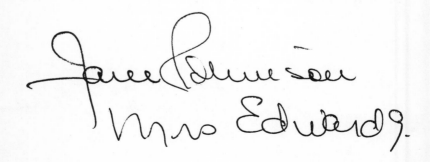

SARA TUCKER'S NOODLE PUDDING

This is my wife's recipe for one of my favorite dishes, which we generally have along with the main course, but which can also be served as a dessert. Made according to the following amounts of ingredients, it should be adequate to serve six or eight.

1 eight-ounce package of egg noodles
4 eggs
½ teaspoon salt
½ cup sugar
½ cup seedless white raisins
2 cooking apples, peeled and sliced
½ cup maraschino cherries, with their syrup

1. Preheat the noodles in salted water according to package directions. Drain and rinse in cold water.

2. Cook the noodles in salted water according to package directions. Drain and rinse in cold water.

3. Add the eggs, salt to taste and sugar (at least half a cup). Add the raisins, apples and cherries. Mix and place in a greased two- quart casserole. Bake one hour.

Serve with chicken or red meat.

Richard Tucker

63

STEPHEN LONGSTREET

NYMPHES DE GRENOUILLES   LONGSTREET

Thia has been in the family for so long we could almost have

invented it . Take 8 pairs of large frog legs <u>with</u> backs . Skin ,

and scald in boiling water . Melt butter in a **large** skillet , and

heat the frog legs . Add a cup of chopped mushrooms , a minced

garlic clove , some chopped chives a small crushed clove , a bit

of chopped parsley . Now <u>sauté</u> and add a cup of chicken

stock , salt , pepper , Cover and cook legs *until they* are tender . Make

a mixture of white wine and flour into a smooth paste , pour over

frog legs . When legs are nearly tender thicken sauce with two egg

yolks beaten with a half cup of cream . Serve with a good

Beaujolais wine

Cordially ,

Stephen Longstreet

1133 Miradero Rd
Beverly Hills , Calif .

64

Executive Mansion
Sacramento
California

OMELETTE WITH MUSHROOMS AND CHEESE

1 can cream of mushroom soup
12 eggs (two eggs per person)
   chopped parsley
   sharp cheddar cheese

Beat eggs well. Stir in soup and chopped
parsley. (No other seasoning necessary).
Melt butter or half bacon grease and half
butter in fry pan, coating bottom and sides
of pan. Pour in egg mixture; reduce heat.
Cook slowly, stirring gently a few times
(do not overstir). As mixture sets, gently
lift eggs from bottom and sides of pan.
Sprinkle grated cheese over eggs while they
are still creamy. Fold over into omelette.
Cook to desired moistness. Serve at once
on a hot platter with fresh sprigs of
parsley.

This is one of our favorite dishes for it
seems to be equally well liked by many
guests the Governor invites to breakfast
at the Mansion.

It can be prepared on a moments notice by
keeping the chopped parsley and grated cheese
readily available in covered containers in
the refrigerator.

Mrs. Edmund G. Brown

From the Desk of . . .

Mrs. Nat Cole

ONE OF MY FAVORITE RECIPES:

SPICED PIGS'FEET

6 pigs' feet
1 tsp.cloves
1 red pepper pod
1 tbsp.paprika
2 cups wine or tarragon
  vinegar
salt and pepper (to taste)

2 bay leaves
1 tsp.dry mustard
1 tsp.celery seed
2 onions
pinch marjoram

Select young,tender pigs' feet. Have them split.
Wash well,cover with cold salted water,and let
soak. Drain. Place in a stew pot. Cover with
cold water and let simmer about 1 hour. Add spices,
vinegar and onions. Simmer slowly until tender.
Serves 6-8.

Serve with a tasty red and green cabbage slaw.

Maria Cole

PETER FALK

Recipe

Pork Chops and Vinegar Peppers

Brown 6 tenderloin pork chops in large frying pan with 1 onion chopped finely. Use $\frac{1}{4}$ cup olive oil for browning.

Remove chops to heavy iron ovenware casserole. Add white vinegar $\frac{1}{4}$ cup to frying pan, stir in all brown bits and add to casserole. Add cracked pepper, very little salt and 1 tsp. thyme. Now add 1 cup water and $\frac{1}{2}$ cup liquid from vinegar peppers.

Bake at 350° 1$\frac{1}{2}$ hrs. Add vinegar peppers, bake 15 min. and serve. Thicken gravy with potato or corn starch.

Potatoes may be added if desired 1 hr before chops are finished. Cut potatoes in quarters for faster cooking.

Peter Falk

67

Dear Dinah:

When it comes to cooking, I can barely make a cup of
tea. But I do have a recipe for millionaires which
I make whenever I can afford it.

All right? Ready? So:

POTATOES ONASSIS

Get yourself a potato and bake it normally.
Is it baked? Okay.

Now open it up and crumple it a bit with your fork.

Now put in a lot of butter -- but hold the salt and
pepper. You'll see why in a moment.

Now put a big, walloping dob of sour cream on it.

Are you still with me? Okay.

Now take 1/4 pound of fresh caviar and put it right
in the middle of the sour cream. That's why you
don't need any salt.

Enormously wealthy people use this as a first
course. In my bracket, I use it as the only course,
with a heart of palm salad and a small glass of
Pouilly Fuisse 1962 -- a dry and slightly heady
wine. Be sure it is served well chilled and drunk
when young. Perhaps it would be wise to have a
little extra on hand for you will find this wine
makes a most agreeable contrast to the spuds.

If you haven't any Pouilly Fuisse 1962, try it with
rye bread and butter and coffee.

Sincerely,

Leonard Spigelgass

P.S.   If you like, add onions, not chives. Chives
are awful. If you want onions, eat onions.

Quick Piquant Sauce

1 can ORTEGA green chile Salsa
1 can chicken gravy (Franco American)
1 can mushroom soup

If you are brave and want it really "hot" eliminate the mushroom soup.

It is great for almost all cooked green vegetables — fish meat — or chicken. You can even jell it in a sea food ring

I blend the ingredients and heat almost to a boil then pour over broccoli — green beans — or spinach. It is at its best on breast of chicken

Rosemary Clooney

69

Bette Davis

Red Flannel Hash

2 cups cooked corn beef,
3 cups cold boiled potatos
1½ cups cooked beets.

chop all these ingredients.
Season and moisten with
cream. Put into hot
buttered ironware frying pan,
stir and spread evenly.
Brown slowly over medium
heat. Serve with poached eggs on top

Bette Davis

dinah shore

ROMAN HOLIDAY DINAH

Cook one package of elbow macaroni in salted water until
just done.
1 lb. of sharp cheddar cheese cut in cubes

Sauce

2 lbs. ground meat (ground chuck or 1 lb. ground chuck and
                    1 lb. hot Italian sausage - if you like)
Small bunch of celery (coarsely cut)
2 cloves of garlic chopped fine
Medium onion (chopped coarsely)
1 green pepper cut in broad strips
6-8 whole mushrooms sliced thin
1 can tomatoes
1 can tomato sauce
Dash of Worcestershire sauce
Pinch of oregano
1 teaspoon of chili powder
Red pepper flakes
1/4 teaspoon cumin

Brown onions and garlic lightly in oil, then add celery
and green pepper. Cook until a little soft. Remove from
pan. Add ground meat to oil and brown well. After meat
is browned, add salt, pepper, chili powder, cumin, worcestershire sauce, oregano (easy on this), mushrooms, onions,
garlic, celery and green pepper. Sprinkle with red pepper
flakes. Add tomatoes and tomato sauce. Allow to cook
slowly for one hour until sauce blends.

Assemble by putting a layer of macaroni in casserole - dot
with butter, add cheese cubes and then a layer of the sauce.
Sprinkle with red pepper flakes. Then another layer of
macaroni, butter and cheese cubes, etc., finishing with a
layer of sauce. Top with grated parmesan or cheddar cheese.
Bake in a 350° oven for 30 minutes until cheese is melted
inside and dish is thoroughly heated. This can be prepared
ahead and reheated 30 minutes before serving.

Serve this with crusty French bread and Italian salad.

dinah shore

ITALIAN SALAD

1 small can of artichoke hearts cut in quarters
1 head of bib lettuce
1/2 cucumber sliced thin
1 green pepper cut in wide strips
1 sweet red onion
1 small can garbanzo beans
4 slices of Italian salami sliced thin
3 fresh mushrooms chopped (optional)
4 radishes sliced thin
1 small tomato quartered

Rub a crystal salad bowl with a cut clove of
garlic. Marinate the cucumbers, green pepper
strips, drained garbanzo beans, artichoke hearts,
radishes and the small tomato in the crystal bowl
in one-half recipe of tart dressing as follows:

6 tablespoons good fresh olive oil
2 tablespoons wine vinegar
1 tablespoon fresh lemon juice
1 teaspoon salt
1/2 teaspoon coarse ground pepper
1 clove garlic pressed

Cover bowl with saran wrap and set in refrigerator
and let it chill a long time.

Just before serving add lettuce, onions, Italian
salami and fresh mushrooms. Sprinkle with a little
salt, accent, fresh coarse ground pepper and a pinch
of tarragon and remainder of dressing. Toss very
lightly. Squeeze a little lemon over salad and
serve ice cold.

ALMOST INSTANT SEAFOOD GUMBO

As our cook has many other interesting
diversions beside cooking, I find myself
regularly cooking - with the approval of
the cook and the alleged approval of my
husband. So, I have to do things fast.
I have measured the time and it is about.
half an hour at the most. Served with
cornbread, it is a main course. (Or with
hot biscuits, a mix) You will notice I
do my own typewriting, too.

2 cans condensed tomato soup
1 quart (or more, depending on guests)
    light cream
1 lb. canned cooked shrimp (or more, if
    you like shrimp)
2 cans crabmeat (7 1/2 ounces each) (bones
    removed)
2 tablespoons Worchestershire sauce
3 teaspoons onion powder
2 teaspoons garlic powder
1 package frozen or fresh okra (sliced)
    cooked according to directions on
    package
2 tablespoons chopped parsley
$\frac{1}{2}$ cup chopped celery, cooked with pepper,
    see following
$\frac{1}{4}$ cup chopped green pepper, sauted in
    bacon fat (see below) to tender
1 crumbled large bayleaf
$\frac{1}{2}$ teaspoon thyme (powdered or dried leaf)
3 slices of bacon, fried crisp, then
    crumbled
2 tablespoons fresh lemon juice (or
    bottled juice. Easier.)   Cont'd.

Seafood Gumbo cont.

Dump the soup, the cream, seafood, and
everything else (prepared as indicated) in
a large pan. Let stand for an hour or so
until flavors are mingled. The longer the
better. If you leave out the cream it can
stand overnight, all to the good. Then add
cream when ready the next day. (Refridge,
if overnight)

Heat thoroughly, but DO NOT BOIL. Serve
in large bowls, with cornbread or hot biscuits.
(Heat the bowls very hot in oven or in hot
water.)

Good for four, six to eight, depending on
appetite. If you wish to thicken, add 2
tablespoons flour to the soup before heat-
ing, but don't add the cream until soup is
thick. And then heat the cream separately,
but not boiling.

Canned shrimp is easy. It is deveined and
needs only rinsing in cold water before
adding to the other ingredients. However,
fresh shrimp or frozen can be used, prepared
in accordance with directions on package,
then added to the soup. This, however, takes
extra time, and who has it? Used canned.

You can't tell this apart from Seafood Gumbo,
Southern style, if you are deft and careful.
But this recipe is fast. The regular takes
two days.

Oh, yes, you can add a little salt and white
pepper, if you need to spark it up, or, at
the very last, 1/2 cup or less of good sherry.
Infinite variety.

Taylor Caldwell

SHELDON LEONARD ENTERPRISES

SEAFOOD GUMBO

With a tossed green salad, and some hot garlic bread, this is a seafood dish which makes a hearty winter dinner.

I have no skill as a cook, but my wife, Frankie, has. I've watched her prepare this often enough to know that she proceeds as follows:

1-1/2 to 2 lbs. shrimp (either cooked or raw)
1 lb. crabmeat
2 cans of clams (whole or pieces)
1 can of pimentos (chopped)
1 large onion (chopped)
1 can of okra or 1 package frozen
2 cans of mushrooms
1 bay leaf
1 green pepper (chopped)
2 cans of tomato sauce
1 lb. can of solid pack tomatoes
4 stalks of celery (chopped)
4 cloves of garlic (crushed)
Handful of parsley (chopped)
1 tbs. gumbo file

Seafood Gumbo cont.

Sauté onion, celery and green pepper in favorite oil
till tender but not brown. Put all liquid ingredients
in a large pot. Add solid pack tomatoes plus an
equal amount of water. Add 2 cans tomato sauce
plus 1 can of water. Add mushrooms (including
liquid), pimento, parsley, bay leaf, crushed
garlic, salt, pepper and the sautéed ingredients.
Bring to a boil and let simmer for 1-1/2 hours.
Add all the seafood and okra. Cook 1 hour longer.
10 minutes before removing from fire, add gumbo
file and stir well. Serve piping hot over rice in
soup dishes. Serves 8 to 10.

Frankie disregards actual quantities of seafood
in preparing this dish, using more of one seafood
and less of another. Also, lobsters or other shellfish can be substituted for crabmeat.

Carolyn Jones

"THAT FISH THING"

1 - Pound	Fresh (not frozen) filet of sole
1 - Pound	Bay shrimp
1 - Medium jar	Mushrooms
1 - Can	Concentrated mushroom soup
1/2-Can	White wine
1/2-Can	Water
1 - Small jar	Chopped pimento
	Fresh dill
	Garlic salt

Lay the filet flat, then take the mushroom caps, chopped pimento, a little fresh dill, bay shrimp, and a tiny bit of garlic salt and put them all on the fish. Then roll the fish up like a blintz and anchor with toothpicks. Place in a baking dish. Mix the mushroom soup with the water and white wine and pour over fish. Bake in 350 degree oven for approximately 25 minutes.

WAFFLES*

1/2 cup butter
1 tablespoon sugar
2 egg yolks
7/8 cup milk, or one cup buttermilk
1 cup and one tablespoon of sifted cake flour
1 pinch salt
2 stiff beaten egg whites
4 teaspoonsful baking powder

Cream butter and sugar, add egg yolks. Beat. Add flour and milk alternately. This may be done at any time. When ready to bake fold in egg whites, and add baking powder.

Mixture should be thick and fluffy

Bake and serve with hot maple syrup and melted butter.

Jacqueline Kennedy

  *Reprinted from "Many Happy Returns" © 1960

Desserts

Dear Abby

ABBY'S PECAN PIE

I cup white Karo syrup
I cup dark brown sugar
I cup (whole) large pecans
I/3 teas. salt
I/3 cup melted butter
I teas. vanilla
3 large eggs

Mix sugar, syrup, butter and salt. Add
slightly beaten eggs and vanilla. Pour
into 9 inch UNBAKED pie shell. Sprinkle
pecans into filling.
Bake at 350 for approximately 45 minutes.

People who fancy real, southern pecan pie
have told me that after trying this recipe
they have thrown all their other pecan pie
recipes away. Nothing tops this one; (not
even whipped cream or ice cream.) Serve it
as is!

Sincerely yours,

Abigail Van Buren

With

Mr Yehudi Menuhin's

Compliments

BIRCHERMEUSLI

2 level tablespoons precooked oatflakes

2 tablespoons brown sugar

Juice of ½ lemon

½ banana (mashed)

2 tablespoons thin cream (or 1 thick)

1 glass jar yoghourt

Juice of 2 oranges

½ grated apple

Berries in season (strawberries, rasp-
    berries, blueberries)

Finely chopped ground almonds

Mix the oatflakes, sugar, lemon juice,
banana and cream and blend well. Add
yoghourt, orange juice and grated apple
immediately into it to prevent browning.
Wash about 1 lb. of whatever berries are
in season and hull them. Mash 3/4 and

continued

add to the mixture. Decorate with the
remaining whole fruit, sprinkle with the
almonds, chill slightly and serve either
in a glass bowl or in individual glass
ice-cream dishes.

This Swiss recipe is particularly delicious in its summer form which I have
given here, but can equally well be eaten
all the year round in a less exciting
style, substituting the berries by 3
grated apples. It can be served as a
breakfast dish or as a dessert, instead
of fresh fruit. One must naturally use
one's judgment with regard to the amount
of sugar or the thickness of the cream,
both these depending upon the particular
quality and choice of fruit used. The
Swiss add a lovely almond puree which can
be bought in Switzerland in tins and is
called "Nuxo". The recipe was invented
by the famous vegetarian doctor, Bircher,
and literally means "Bircher-porridge"
and is as healthy as it is delicious.

Mrs. Joseph P. Kennedy

BOSTON CREAM PIE

Bake a cake in two seven-inch or eight-inch layer cake tins, using a cake mix or Boston Favorite Cake, one egg, or Golden layer cake recipe. Put the layers together with whipped cream, Cream filling, or Rich Cream Filling. Sprinkle top with confectioners' sugar or spread with Chocolate Frosting.

Recipe for Boston Favorite Cake:

> (Set oven at 375 degrees for layers. If all-purpose flour is used, reduce amount by two tablespoons)

Sift together: 1 3/4 cups pastry or cake flour

½ teaspoon salt

2 teaspoons baking powder

Cream thoroughly 1/3 cup butter or margarine

Add ½ teaspoon vanilla

Beat in gradually 1 cup sugar

Beat until fluffy, then beat in 2 egg yolks

Stir in ½ cup of the flour mixture

Stir in ¼ cup milk.   Add ½ cup of the flour mixture and ¼ cup milk

Add rest of the flour mixture and beat just enough to blend well

cont.

Beat until they stand up in soft peaks -- 2 egg whites
Fold into the batter. Spoon into the pans. Bake layers
20 to 30 minutes.

To make with an electric mixer or beater, do not separate
the eggs. Add to the creamed butter and sugar one at
a time, beating well.

Recipe for the Cream Filling:

Put in a small heavy pan: 1/2 cup sugar

3 teaspoons flour or 1
tablespoon cornstarch

Few grains salt

Stir in 1 cup milk

Cook and stir over low heat until the mixture thickens
(about 5 minutes)

Add: 1 egg or 2 egg yolks, slightly beaten

Cook and stir 3 minutes longer   -   Chill and flavor

Recipe for Chocolate Frosting:

Put in top of a double boiler: 2 ounces unsweetened
chocolate

1 tablespoon butter

1/2 cup milk

Cook until the chocolate melts - stir well

Let stand until lukewarm

Stir in: 2 cups confectioners' sugar
            1/2 teaspoon vanilla

Beat until thick enough to spread

CHOCOLATE ROLL

6   Tablespoons of Cocoa
6   Tablespoons of Flour   Sifted together

1/2 Teaspoon of Baking Powder

1/4 Teaspoon of Salt

4   Eggs Beaten Separately

1   Teaspoon vanilla

3/4 Cup of Sugar

Beat the egg yolks well with sugar. Add the sifted flour and cocoa. Fold in the beaten whites of the egg. Bake at 400 degrees for 12 minutes. Cook in a well greased pan.

Mrs. Robert Kennedy

A Light Coffee Cake

1 cup Sugar	2 tsps. Baking powder
1½ Cups flour (Sifted)	½ Cup Butter (¼ lb.)
½ tsp. Salt	2 eggs (Separated)
½ cup milk	1 tsp. Vanilla
	1 tsp. Lemon Juice or extract

Cream Butter and Sugar. Add egg yolks, one at a time. Sift flour, baking powder & salt. Add milk and flour alternately to first mixture. Add stiffly beaten egg whites. Add flavoring. Then bake in 9 inch pan in slow oven (350°F) for 45 minutes. (Grease bottom of pan — then cut circular piece of wax paper to fit bottom, grease that and dust with flour. Julie Harris

Ida Lupino Duff

A RICH FRUITCAKE

12 oz Butter
12 oz Sugar
1lb   Flour
6 Eggs
12oz currants
12oz golden raisins
12 oz dark raisins
4oz cherries
 4oz mixed peel
2 Tablespoons sherry or milk
1 level teaspoon mixed spice
1 level teaspoon cocoa

cake tin nine inches square lined and greased

sift the flour, mixed spice and cocoa very well
   together into a basin. in another basin, mix the
currants, sultanas raisins, chopped peel and cherries

   beat thebutter to a soft cream add the sugar and
beat the mixture   till it is soft and creamy.
beat the eggs well together.
   add the beaten eggs a little at a time to the creamed
mixture beating it well.
   lightly stir in flour alternately with the sherry.
   lastly stir in the fruit.

   turn the mixture into the prepared tin, press
into the corners, then smooth over the surface and
   slightly hollow out the centre.

   bake at 325 for an hour. lower to 300 and bake for
   her and half to two hours
   test the cake after the hour and half when ready
   cool on wire tray remove greased paper.
   this cake improves with keeping in airtight tin .

Janet Leigh

Dear Dinah,

    In spite of its fancy name, this is
really an old-fashioned yellow cake, the
kind that goes so well with homemade ice-
cream.

GATEAU DORE

½ cup of butter
1 cup of sugar
2 cups of cake flour
3 teaspoons baking powder
Yolks of four eggs
½ cup of milk

Preheat oven to 350 degrees, a moderate oven.
Cream butter well, add sugar, continue beating,
add yolks beaten light, add 1 teaspoon vanilla,
mix thoroughly, then add milk alternately with
the flour and baking powder mixed. Beat, place
in greased and floured pan, bake 35 to 45
minutes. Bake in loaf or layers.

Janet Leigh

BOB HOPE

NAME OF RECIPE: BOB HOPE'S FAVORITE LEMON PIE

INGREDIENTS:

1 Cup Sugar plus 2 Tbsp.
3 Tbsp. Corn Starch
1 Cup Boiling Water
4 Tbsp. Lemon Juice
2 Tbsp. Butter
4 Egg Yolks
Pinch of Salt ....Grated rind of 1 lemon

PREPARATION:

Combine corn starch and sugar, add water slowly,
stirring constantly, until thick and smooth. Add
slightly beaten egg yolks, butter, lemon rind and
juice, and salt. Cook 2 or 3 minutes. Pour into
baked shell. Cover with meringue made from 3 egg
whites beaten stiff, and 2½ tbsp. sugar. Bake in
slow oven 15 minutes, or until light brown.

Mocha Surprise

1 Sq. Chocolate
2 Tb. Butter
½ cup Milk

1 Tb. Vanilla
3/4 cup Sugar
1 cup Flour

2 Tb. Baking Powder

Topping:

½ cup Brown Sugar
4 Tb. Cocoa

½ cup White Sugar

Melt chocolate and butter. Add milk and vanilla.
Sift and mix in sugar, flour and baking powder.
Pour into baking pan. Mix and sprinkle topping
over top. Pour cold coffee over all. Bake 1/4
hour in 350° oven. Best served while still warm.

***

This is one of our favorites.

Desilu Productions Inc.

780 NORTH GOWER STREET • HOLLYWOOD 38 • CALIFORNIA

HOLLYWOOD 9-5911

LUCILLE BALL
PRESIDENT

CABLE ADDRESS
"DESILU"

PERSIMMON CAKE

2 Cups sugar) Creamed together
3 Tablespoons butter)

2 Cups persimmon pulp
2 Cups chopped walnut meats
1 Cup seedless raisins
1 Cup dates - cut fine
Rind of 1 orange - grated

1 Cup Milk
4 Cups Cake flour - sifted

2 Teaspoons Cinnamon
1/2 teaspoon Cloves
1/2 teaspoon Allspice
1/2 teaspoon Nutmeg
1/4 teaspoon Soda
3 teaspoons baking powder
2 teaspoons vanilla extract

Bake in 2 large loaf tins or 4 small loaf tins.
(Batter can also be dropped from a spoon on
cookie sheets for cookies.)

Bake 300 degrees for 1 and 1/2 hours.

91

Shoo Fly Pie - (Pennsylvania Dutch)

1/2 Cup boiling water
1/2 Cup dark molasses
1 egg yolk, well beaten
1/2 teaspoon soda
1/2 Cup brown sugar, packed
1/4 Cup margarine (1/2 cube)
1/4 teaspoon salt
1/8 teaspoon nutmeg
1/8 teaspoon cloves
1/8 teaspoon ginger
1/2 teaspoon cinnamon
1 unbaked pie shell (9 or 10 minutes)

In the boiling water, put molasses, beaten egg yolk and baking soda and combine all thoroughly. Mix into the flour all the other ingredients and work it with your fingers until it is all crumbly. Put into unbaked pie shell, first some molasses mixture, then top that with some crumbs, making alternate layers ending with crumbs on top. Bake in preheated oven 350° until crust is well browned and filling is firm (45 to 50 minutes). Whipped cream is great on this

Edie Adams

SANDY KOUFAX

Dear Dinah,

Thank you for the offer to publish my favorite recipe, but there is one problem. I don't cook!

Boiling water for coffee just doesn't require a recipe.

Sincerely,

Sandy Koufax